Contents

Y0-BXS-174

Useful facts and figures

Note on metrication

In this book quantities are given in both Imperial and metric measures. Exact conversion from Imperial to metric does not always give very convenient working quantities so for greater convenience and ease of working we have taken an equivalent of 25 grammes/millilitres to the ounce/fluid ounce. 1 oz. is exactly 28·35 g. and $\frac{1}{4}$ pint (5 fl. oz.) is 142 ml., so you will see that by using the unit of 25 you will get a slightly smaller result than the Imperial measures would give.

Occasionally, for example in a basic recipe such as a Victoria sandwich made with 4 oz. flour, butter and sugar and 2 eggs, we have rounded the conversion up to give a more generous result. For larger amounts where the exact conversion is not critical, for instance in soups or stews, we have used kilogrammes and fractions (1 kg. equals 2·2 lb.) and litres and fractions (1 litre equals 1·76 pints). All recipes have been individually converted so that each recipe preserves the correct proportions.

Oven temperatures

The following chart gives the Celsius (Centigrade) equivalents recommended by the Electricity Council.

Description	Fahrenheit	Celsius	Gas Mark
Very cool	225	110	$\frac{1}{4}$
	250	130	$\frac{1}{2}$
Cool	275	140	1
	300	150	2
Moderate	325	170	3
	350	180	4
Moderately hot	375	190	5
	400	200	6
Hot	425	220	7
	450	230	8
Very hot	475	240	9

Introduction

Everyone enjoys entertaining and whether you are giving a dinner party in the grand style or a lunch party for two, you will find this collection of recipes an invaluable help.

I have included recipes for starters, fish dishes, main courses and desserts and, of course, there is a colour picture to show you how each finished dish will look — a tremendous asset when you are planning a party as you want to make sure that you have a good variety of colour in your dishes.

From the recipes I have given you will be able to plan many types of parties and if you are giving a buffet party there are some one-dish recipes which are ideal for this type of entertaining — try for example La daube provençale and serve it with a selection of salads. Remember that food for this type of party needs to be easy to manage with just a fork. The serving quantities for each recipe are given and if you are giving a large party it will be quite easy to double or treble the quantities.

A final word on entertaining — try to get as much preparation as possible done beforehand and leave plenty of time to get yourself ready for the party. If you have a freezer you will find some of the recipes are suitable for freezing.

Marguerite Patten

Vichyssoise soup

Cooking time: 45 minutes
Preparation time: 15 minutes
Main cooking utensils: large saucepan, sieve, ovenproof dish
Serves: 4–6

Imperial	Metric
4 medium-sized leeks	4 medium-sized leeks
2 oz. butter or margarine	50 g. butter or margarine
3 small potatoes	3 small potatoes
$\frac{1}{4}$ pint water	125 ml. water
1 pint chicken stock, or water and chicken stock cube	generous $\frac{1}{2}$ litre chicken stock, or water and chicken stock cube
1 level teaspoon salt	1 level teaspoon salt
pinch pepper	pinch pepper
$\frac{1}{4}$ pint thick cream	125 ml. thick cream
To garnish:	*To garnish:*
chopped chives or spring onion tops	chopped chives or spring onion tops

1. Use the white part of the leeks only, wash well and chop.
2. Melt the butter in a pan and cook the leeks slowly for 10–15 minutes, without letting them brown.
3. Peel the potatoes and cut in cubes.
4. Add to the leeks with the water and stock.
5. Season, cover pan and simmer for 25 minutes until the potatoes are soft.
6. Rub the mixture through a sieve, return to the pan, add the cream and heat, but do not boil.
7. Serve either hot or chilled and sprinkled with chopped chives or finely cut spring onion tops.

Note: Store in the refrigerator. If reheating, do so gently.

Variation
Add 1 small onion, chopped. If serving cold, use $\frac{1}{4}$ pint (125 ml.) white wine in place of water.

Cucumber soup

Cooking time: 30 minutes
Preparation time: 15 minutes
Main cooking utensils: large saucepan, sieve
Serves: 4

Imperial	Metric
1 pint white stock or water and chicken stock cube	generous $\frac{1}{2}$ litre white stock or water and chicken stock cube
1 small cucumber	1 small cucumber
1 small onion	1 small onion
1 oz. fat	25 g. fat
1½ oz. flour	40 g. flour
seasoning	seasoning
¼ pint milk	125 ml. milk
green colouring	green colouring
To garnish:	*To garnish:*
parsley	parsley
slices of cucumber	slices of cucumber
croûtons (see note)	croûtons (see note)

1. Bring the stock to the boil.

2. Cut 4 slices cucumber for garnish, peel remainder, cut into ½-inch (1-cm.) slices.

3. Chop the onion, add the cucumber and onion to the stock.

4. Cook gently until the cucumber is soft, rub through a hair sieve.

5. Melt the fat in the same saucepan, blend in the flour and cook for 2–3 minutes.

6. Add the sieved cucumber gradually, stirring all the time. Bring to the boil and cook for 5 minutes.

7. Season and add the milk, reheat but do not boil.

8. Colour with a few drops of green colouring.

9. Serve sprinkled with chopped parsley and slices of cucumber. Serve croûtons separately.

Note: To make croûtons, cut 2–3 slices bread into small dice. Fry in hot fat until brown, drain on absorbent paper.

Variations
Leek soup: Use 4 large leeks instead of cucumber.

Cauliflower soup: Use cauliflower florets from 1 cauliflower instead of cucumber.

Liver loaf

Cooking time: 1½ hours
Preparation time: 25 minutes
Main cooking utensils: 2-lb. (1-kg.) loaf tin, roasting tin
Oven temperature: very moderate (350°F., 180°C., Gas Mark 3—4)
Oven position: centre
Serves: 6—8

Imperial	Metric
1–1¼ lb. calves' or pigs' liver	500–600 g. calves' or pigs' liver
4 oz. salt pork or fat bacon	100 g. salt pork or fat bacon
4 anchovy fillets (optional)	4 anchovy fillets (optional)
1 small onion	1 small onion
1 clove garlic	1 clove garlic
2 oz. soft breadcrumbs	50 g. soft breadcrumbs
seasoning	seasoning
2 small eggs, or 1 whole egg and 1 egg yolk	2 small eggs, or 1 whole egg and 1 egg yolk
12 rashers thin, long streaky bacon	12 rashers thin, long streaky bacon
To garnish:	*To garnish:*
gherkin	gherkin
canned or home-made potato salad	canned or home-made potato salad
chives	chives

1. Slice the liver and put it through the mincer with the pork and anchovies.

2. Add the chopped onion and crushed clove garlic to the liver etc. and put it through the mincer again (for a fine pâté put it through twice).

3. Blend with the breadcrumbs, seasoning and eggs, and mix very thoroughly.

4. Line the tin with most of the rashers and put in the mixture, pressing down firmly.

5. Cover with the rest of the bacon rashers cut into halves.

6. Stand in a tin of cold water, and bake until firm.

7. When cooked put a piece of foil or greaseproof paper and a weight on top and leave until cold.

8. Serve garnished with gherkin. Slice, and serve with potato salad, chives and a mixed salad.

Note: Store covered, in the refrigerator.

Variation

Serve with hot toast as an hors d'oeuvre (in which case it will serve up to 12 portions).

Smoked haddock pâté

Cooking time: 10 minutes
Preparation time: 15 minutes
Main cooking utensils: saucepan, sieve
Serves: 6–8

Imperial	Metric
12 oz. smoked haddock	300 g. smoked haddock
2 oz. butter	50 g. butter
12 tablespoons double cream	12 tablespoons double cream
pepper	pepper
cayenne pepper	cayenne pepper
2 teaspoons lemon juice	2 teaspoons lemon juice
1 teaspoon Worcestershire sauce	1 teaspoon Worcestershire sauce
2 oz. butter, melted	50 g. butter, melted
To garnish:	*To garnish:*
lemon	lemon
parsley	parsley

1. Wipe the fish, poach in boiling water for 10 minutes.
2. Drain the fish, skin and flake.
3. Mash the fish and pass it through a sieve then blend with the butter (or blend in the liquidiser) to make a purée.
4. Whip the cream until almost thick, fold in the fish and season well, tasting as you go, add lemon juice and Worcestershire sauce.
5. Pour into a dish or individual serving dishes and allow to set.
6. Cover the top of the pâté with melted butter and leave to set.
7. Garnish with lemon and parsley and serve with hot toast and butter.

Variations

Use smoked cod's roe, or white fish and extra seasoning.
Kipper pâté: Use flesh from 4 lightly cooked kippers, flake and sieve, blend with 2 oz. (50 g.) butter, pepper, 2 teaspoons lemon juice, 1 teaspoon chopped parsley, 1 teaspoon Worcestershire sauce. If liked, add 1 oz. (25 g.) grated Parmesan cheese.

Mixed hors d'oeuvre

A simple selection of ingredients, as in the picture, make a delicious hors d'oeuvre.

Arrange them in individual dishes on a tray or in lines on a large dish, so that it is easy for everyone to help themselves.

All foods should have dressing with them, so no extra oil or vinegar or mayonnaise need be served. (For French dressing, see page 33; for mayonnaise, see page 29.)

Russian salad
Mix cooked diced fresh vegetables or canned vegetables or frozen vegetables with mayonnaise. To make a more unusual salad, chopped hard-boiled eggs and chopped ham may be blended with the vegetables.

Salami
A selection of salami should be sliced neatly; rings of raw onion and watercress sprigs are a colourful garnish.

Potato salad
Dice cooked potatoes while hot, mix with mayonnaise and grated raw onion or chopped spring onion or chives. Chopped parsley, diced gherkin, capers may also be included and a garnish of paprika pepper and chopped parsley give colour. Add chopped celery and chopped green pepper for a more interesting salad.

Gherkins, sliced cucumber tossed in French dressing, sliced or whole stuffed, green or black olives are generally included in hors d'oeuvres.

Rollmop or Bismarck herrings, bought in jars if wished, should be topped with rings of raw onion and sprinkled with parsley.

Egg mayonnaise
Coat whole or halved hard-boiled eggs with mayonnaise, top with chopped parsley and paprika pepper; or fill the whites of hard-boiled eggs with shrimps, prawns, crab meat, etc., blended with mayonnaise and topped with sieved egg yolk.

Beetroot, tomato, sardines, sweetcorn, shrimps or prawns can also be added.

Melon and ham cornets

Preparation time: 15 minutes
Main utensils: mixing bowl, cocktail sticks
Serves: 4

Imperial	Metric
½ large or 1 small melon	½ large or 1 small melon
3–4 tablespoons mayonnaise	3–4 tablespoons mayonnaise
1 tablespoon lemon juice	1 tablespoon lemon juice
seasoning	seasoning
shake of sugar	shake of sugar
approximately 12 thin slices cooked ham	approximately 12 thin slices cooked ham
To garnish:	*To garnish:*
prawns	prawns
parsley	parsley

1. Remove the flesh from the melon and cut it into small dice.
2. Blend with the rest of the ingredients, except the ham, add sugar and seasoning to taste.
3. Form the ham into cornet shapes, securing these with cocktail sticks.
4. Arrange on a flat dish and fill with the melon mixture.
5. Garnish with prawns and parsley.
6. Serve for a buffet meal, with extra mayonnaise and a green salad, if liked.

Variations

Use diced pineapple in place of melon. Use canned chopped ham, salami, tongue or garlic sausage in place of the ham.

Prawn cocktail with soured cream sauce

Preparation time: 10 minutes
Main utensils: sharp knife, basin
Serves: 4

Imperial

½ lettuce
6 oz. shelled prawns
1 tablespoon fresh tomato purée
    (skin tomatoes, then rub
    through a sieve)
few drops Worcestershire sauce
seasoning
1 carton soured cream or
    ¼ pint fresh cream and
    1 tablespoon lemon juice
paprika (optional)
To garnish:
4 whole prawns
4 lemon slices

Metric

½ lettuce
150 g. shelled prawns
1 tablespoon fresh tomato purée
    (skin tomatoes, then rub
    though a sieve)
few drops Worcestershire sauce
seasoning
1 carton soured cream or
    125 ml. fresh cream and
    1 tablespoon lemon juice
paprika (optional)
To garnish:
4 whole prawns
4 lemon slices

1. Shred the lettuce finely and divide this and the shelled prawns between four glasses.

2. Blend together the tomato purée, Worcestershire sauce, seasoning and soured cream.

3. To serve, pour the sauce over the prawns and lettuce just before serving. Sprinkle with paprika if wished. Garnish with whole prawns and lemon slices, slit halfway up between the skin and the flesh so that they sit on the edge of the glass.

Note: This dish is low in calories and therefore suitable for those on a diet.

Variations

Use other shellfish or flaked steamed white fish; if using this add a little anchovy essence which gives both additional colour and flavour. Shredded endive could be used in place of lettuce but it has a slightly more bitter flavour.

Cheese aigrettes

Cooking time: few minutes and 4–5 minutes for frying
Preparation time: 15 minutes
Main cooking utensils: saucepan, pan for oil
Makes: about 24 cocktails-size aigrettes

Imperial	**Metric**
3 tablespoons corn oil	3 tablespoons corn oil
$\frac{1}{4}$ pint water	125 ml. water
2$\frac{1}{2}$ oz. plain flour	65 g. plain flour
$\frac{1}{2}$ oz. cornflour	15 g. cornflour
good pinch salt	good pinch salt
shake pepper	shake pepper
shake cayenne pepper	shake cayenne pepper
2 eggs	2 eggs
2 oz. Cheddar or Parmesan cheese, finely grated	50 g. Cheddar or Parmesan cheese, finely grated
good 1 pint corn oil for frying	generous $\frac{1}{2}$ litre corn oil for frying
To garnish:	*To garnish:*
little grated Cheddar cheese	little grated Cheddar cheese
parsley	parsley

1. Put oil and water into the saucepan and bring to the boil.
2. Remove from the heat and gradually stir in flour and corn-flour, sieved with the seasonings.
3. Beat well and return to a low heat, stirring until the mixture forms a dry ball and leaves the sides of the pan quite clean.
4. Remove from heat once again, cool slightly and beat in the eggs.
5. Lastly stir in the grated cheese.
6. Heat the oil to 375°F. (190°C.), or until a cube of stale bread goes golden brown in just under 30 seconds.
7. Drop spoonfuls of the mixture into the hot oil and fry until crisp and brown.
8. Drain on crumpled tissue or kitchen paper and garnish with cheese and parsley. Serve hot.

Variation
Add 1 oz. (25 g.) finely chopped nuts at stage 5.

Chicken balls and mustard dip

Cooking time: 15 minutes
Preparation time: 20 minutes
Main cooking utensils: saucepan, frying pan
Serves: 4–8 (8 if served as a meal starter and followed by a substantial main dish)

Imperial	Metric
3 oz. fine semolina	75 g. fine semolina
¾ pint chicken stock, or	scant ½ litre chicken stock, or
water and chicken stock cube	water and chicken stock cube
8 oz. cooked chicken	200 g. cooked chicken
8 oz. cooked ham	200 g. cooked ham
1 teaspoon chopped parsley	1 teaspoon chopped parsley
seasoning	seasoning
Coating:	*Coating:*
1 egg	1 egg
1½-2 oz. fine semolina	40–50 g. fine semolina
To fry:	*To fry:*
1 lb. fat or 1 pint oil	½ kg. fat or ½ litre oil
Mustard dip:	*Mustard dip:*
¼ pint thick cream	125 ml. thick cream
1 tablespoon French mustard	1 tablespoon French mustard

1. Blend the fine semolina with the chicken stock.

2. Bring to the boil, stirring continuously.

3. Simmer for 2 minutes, stirring well.

4. Add the finely chopped or minced chicken, ham and the parsley.

5. Season well, allow to cool and become firm (see note).

6. Roll into very small balls and brush with beaten egg. Then coat in semolina.

7. Fry in very hot fat or oil until golden brown.

8. Drain on absorbent paper and serve with the mustard dip.

9. Make the mustard dip by blending the whipped cream and mustard.

Note: The chicken balls can be stored overnight in the refrigerator before coating.

Variation

Use turkey instead of chicken. These are also suitable as a cocktail snack. Form into hazelnut-sized balls, fry as above and serve on cocktail sticks. Arrange them around the bowl of dip.

Cheese straws

Cooking time: 8–10 minutes
Preparation time: 15 minutes
Main cooking utensils: baking trays
Oven temperature: hot (425–450°F., 220–230°C., Gas Mark 7–8)
Oven position: near top
Makes: approximately 48

Imperial	Metric
8 oz. plain flour	200 g. plain flpur
good pinch salt	good pinch salt
shake pepper	shake pepper
pinch dry mustard	pinch dry mustard
shake celery salt	shake celery salt
5 oz. butter	125 g. butter
4 oz. firm Cheddar cheese, very finely grated	100 g. firm Cheddar cheese, very finely grated
2 egg yolks	2 egg yolks
To glaze:	*To glaze:*
2 egg whites	2 egg whites

1. Sieve the flour and seasonings.

2. Rub in the butter until the mixture resembles fine bread-crumbs; add the cheese.

3. Bind with egg yolks, knead lightly.

4. Roll out firmly, but gently on a lightly floured board until about a $\frac{1}{4}$ inch ($\frac{1}{2}$ cm.) in thickness.

5. Cut into very narrow fingers.

6. Re-roll any pastry left and make into rings and extra fingers.

7. Put on to lightly greased baking trays and brush with the lightly beaten egg white.

8. Bake until crisp and golden brown.

9. As these are very fragile allow to cool on the baking tray for a few minutes, then transfer to a wire tray to finish cooling.

10. Serve the straws through the rings or place in tall glasses. These are ideal to serve at a cocktail party.

Note: Store in an airtight tin.

Variations

Cut the straws a little thicker, then twist before baking. Or, when cooled dip each end in mayonnaise, or one end in paprika pepper and the other in finely chopped parsley.

Star apple salad

Preparation time: 10 minutes plus time for making mayonnaise
Main utensil: sharp knife
Serves: 4

Imperial	Metric
3 oz. black grapes	75 g. black grapes
3 oz. green grapes	75 g. green grapes
3 eating apples	3 eating apples
1 lemon	1 lemon
2 celery stalks	2 celery stalks
2 oz. walnuts	50 g. walnuts
mayonnaise (see stage 6)	mayonnaise (see stage 6)
To garnish:	*To garnish:*
parsley	parsley

1. Wash and dry the black grapes and remove the pips — do this with a very fine hair pin or pin (see page 87).

2. Skin the green grapes and remove pips.

3. Chop two of the apples, but cut the third into slices to form the star, sprinkle with the lemon juice to keep them white.

4. Chop the celery neatly and the walnuts coarsely.

5. Mix ingredients together, put into a bowl, top with apple slices.

6. Serve with mayonnaise, cheese or ham or other cold meat. Garnish with parsley. (To make mayonnaise, blend an egg yolk with a pinch of salt, pepper, mustard and sugar. Add about 1 teaspoon vinegar or lemon juice, then gradually blend in $\frac{1}{4}-\frac{1}{2}$ pint (125–250 ml.) oil, drop by drop, beating well with a wooden spoon to give a smooth sauce.)

Note: Diced apples can be added to a green or mixed salad.

Variation
Use pineapple instead of grapes.

Green pepper and tomato salad

Main utensil: sharp knife
Serves: 4

Imperial	Metric
2 green peppers	2 green peppers
1 lb. tomatoes	½ kg. tomatoes
4–5 spring onions or 1 small onion	4–5 spring onions or 1 small onion
little basil	little basil
Oil and vinegar dressing:	*Oil and vinegar dressing:*
½–1 level teaspoon mustard	½–1 level teaspoon mustard
good pinch salt	good pinch salt
good pinch pepper	good pinch pepper
good pinch sugar	good pinch sugar
3 tablespoons olive oil	3 tablespoons olive oil
1½ tablespoons vinegar	1½ tablespoons vinegar

1. Cut the green peppers into neat rings, discard the seeds and core.

2. Cut the tomatoes and onions into thin rings.

3. Arrange in a shallow dish.

4. For dressing, blend seasonings and sugar, gradually work in oil and the vinegar.

5. Add the basil to the dressing.

6. Pour dressing over salad.

7. Serve with chicken or meat dishes or as an hors d'oeuvre.

Note: Many people like to blanch peppers, to soften them, before adding to a salad. Put the peppers into boiling salted water for about 4 minutes. Drain, cool, then prepare as stage 1.

Variation

Add a little crushed garlic.

Italian rice salad

Cooking time: 20–25 minutes
Preparation time: 15 minutes
Main cooking utensils: saucepan, frying pan
Serves: 4

Imperial	Metric
8 oz. long-grain rice	200 g. long-grain rice
2 green peppers	2 green peppers
8 oz. tomatoes	200 g. tomatoes
1 aubergine	1 aubergine
2 tablespoons oil	2 tablespoons oil
French dressing:	*French dressing:*
$\frac{1}{2}$ teaspoon salt	$\frac{1}{2}$ teaspoon salt
$\frac{1}{4}$ teaspoon pepper	$\frac{1}{4}$ teaspoon pepper
$\frac{1}{4}$ teaspoon dry mustard	$\frac{1}{4}$ teaspoon dry mustard
1 tablespoon vinegar	1 tablespoon vinegar
2 tablespoons oil	2 tablespoons oil

1. Cook the rice in boiling salted water, until just soft.
2. Rinse in cold water and drain thoroughly.
3. Shred the peppers, discard the core and seeds, peel and slice the tomatoes, slice the aubergine (do not peel).
4. Fry the peppers, tomatoes and aubergine in oil until soft — do not overcook.
5. Add the cooked rice and stir over a low heat for a few minutes.
6. To make the dressing, put the salt, pepper and mustard in a bowl, or on a plate.
7. Blend in the vinegar and oil gradually until smooth.
8. Add the rice and vegetables and toss well in the dressing.
9. Serve as cold as possible.

Variations
A little diced ham may be added if wished, or add grated cheese or cooked peas and grated raw carrot. Add a pinch of sugar to the dressing if liked.

Apple and prawn salad

Preparation time: 15 minutes
Main utensils: bowl, 4 scallop shells
Serves: 4

Imperial	**Metric**
6 oz. cooked rice	150 g. cooked rice
2 tomatoes	2 tomatoes
2 small red eating apples	2 small red eating apples
1 green pepper	1 green pepper
1 stick celery	1 stick celery
seasoning	seasoning
French dressing (see page 33)	French dressing (see page 33)
4 oz. peeled prawns	100 g. peeled prawns
To garnish:	*To garnish:*
parsley	parsley
prawns	prawns

1. Mix together the cooked rice, (rinse in cold water, then dry — this removes surplus starch), skinned chopped tomatoes and diced apple.
2. Dice the pepper — remove core and seeds — dice celery and add to the rice.
3. Season well and add the dressing.
4. Pile in scallop shells and top with peeled prawns.
5. Garnish with chopped parsley and whole prawns.
6. Serve as an hors d'oeuvre or light supper dish.

Note : If frozen prawns are used, allow to defrost slowly at room temperature before using.

Variations
Use diced cheese or flaked crab meat instead of the prawns.

Devilled egg salad

Cooking time: 10 minutes
Preparation time: 10 minutes
Main cooking utensil: saucepan
Serves: 4

Imperial	**Metric**
4 eggs	4 eggs
3 tablespoons mayonnaise	3 tablespoons mayonnaise
1–2 teaspoons curry powder	1–2 teaspoons curry powder
few drops Worcestershire sauce	few drops Worcestershire sauce
1 tablespoon chutney (optional) or 1 tablespoon chopped cocktail onions	1 tablespoon chutney (optional) or 1 tablespoon chopped cocktail onions
To garnish:	*To garnish:*
lettuce or endive	lettuce or endive
tomato	tomato
cucumber	cucumber

1. Hard-boil the eggs, cut in half lengthways, remove the yolk while still warm, and mash or sieve.
2. Blend with the rest of the ingredients, pile into the egg white cases.
3. Serve on a bed of lettuce or endive. Garnish with pieces of tomato and thin slices of cucumber.

Note: To hard-boil eggs cook them for approximately 10 minutes in boiling salted water — immediately plunge them into cold water and crack the shells. This prevents a dark line forming around the yolk.

Variation
Stuffed eggs: Blend yolk with mayonnaise as above, but omit other ingredients and substitute chopped prawns or grated cheese or chopped ham or chopped chicken.

Fried scampi

Cooking time: see stage 4
Preparation time: few minutes, plus time for fish to defrost, see
stage 1
Main cooking utensils: frying pan, or pan and wire basket
for deep frying
Serves: 4

Imperial	Metric
approximately 24 scampi	approximately 24 scampi
Coating:	*Coating:*
1 egg	1 egg
1 tablespoon water	1 tablespoon water
3 tablespoons crisp breadcrumbs (raspings)	3 tablespoons crisp breadcrumbs (raspings)
fat or oil for frying	fat or oil for frying
To garnish:	*To garnish:*
lemon	lemon
parsley	parsley
Tartare sauce:	*Tartare sauce:*
$\frac{1}{2}$ tablespoon chopped capers	$\frac{1}{2}$ tablespoon chopped capers
$\frac{1}{2}$ tablespoon chopped parsley	$\frac{1}{2}$ tablespoon chopped parsley
$\frac{1}{2}$ tablespoon chopped gherkins	$\frac{1}{2}$ tablespoon chopped gherkins
little lemon juice	little lemon juice
$\frac{1}{4}$ pint mayonnaise (see page 29)	125 ml. mayonnaise (see page 29)

1. Although the scampi can be cooked if still frozen it is better to allow frozen scampi to defrost completely if frying, so they may be drained of any surplus moisture and then coated.

2. If using cooked scampi, shell, then coat in the egg and crumbs.

3. To coat the fish, blend the egg with the water to give a lighter coating, then dip in the breadcrumbs; shake off any surplus.

4. Fry in the hot fat or oil; allow about 3—4 minutes for uncooked fish, but just under the 3 minutes for cooked fish.

5. Drain on crumpled tissue paper or kitchen paper, then garnish with the lemon, cut into wedges or half slices, and parsley. Serve with tartare sauce made by blending the capers and other ingredients with the mayonnaise.

Variations

Fry the scampi in butter without coating them.

Scampi provençale: Fry 1 finely chopped onion, 1 clove garlic in 2 oz. (50 g.) butter, add 3 skinned chopped tomatoes, then the scampi and heat well.

King crab mayonnaise

Cooking time: 10–15 minutes
Preparation time: 10–20 minutes (depending on whether fresh or
    frozen crab is used)
Main cooking utensil: saucepan
Serves: 6

Imperial	Metric
1 medium-sized onion	1 medium-sized onion
1 tablespoon oil	1 tablespoon oil
1 dessertspoon curry powder	1 dessertspoon curry powder
1 dessertspoon tomato purée	1 dessertspoon tomato purée
1 tablespoon clear honey	1 tablespoon clear honey
1 wineglas red wine	1 wineglass red wine
$\frac{3}{4}$ wineglass water	$\frac{3}{4}$ wineglass water
seasoning	seasoning
juice of $\frac{1}{2}$ lemon	juice of $\frac{1}{2}$ lemon
$\frac{1}{2}$ pint mayonnaise (see page 29)	250 ml. mayonnaise (see page 29)
1 lb. frozen crab meat or 1 large crab	$\frac{1}{2}$ kg. frozen crab meat or 1 large crab
To garnish:	*To garnish:*
3–4 tomatoes	3–4 tomatoes
few black olives	few black olives

1. Fry the chopped onion in oil for 3–4 minutes.

2. Add the curry powder and cook for a further 2 minutes.

3. Add the tomato purée, honey, wine and water. Bring to the boil, season and add lemon juice.

4. Simmer until it has become thick and syrupy. Strain and leave to cool. Stir into the mayonnaise and crab meat.

5. Arrange in a long shallow dish and garnish with tomato and black olives. Serve with a green salad.

Note: If using a fresh crab, pull the body away from the shell, remove the meat from the body, discard the stomach bag and the grey parts (dead men's fingers), remove the meat from the crushed claws also. Serve dark and light meat separately, or mix together as in this salad.

Dressed lobster

Preparation time: 15 minutes
Serves: 2

Imperial	Metric
1 medium-sized hen or cock lobster	1 medium-sized hen or cock lobster
To garnish:	*To garnish:*
small portion cucumber	small portion cucumber
1–2 tomatoes	1–2 tomatoes
lettuce	lettuce
watercress	watercress

1. To judge a good lobster it should feel heavy for its size. If it is large but unexpectedly light, it is full of water.

2. Plunge the lobster into boiling water and cook gently for 20 minutes for lobsters up to 1 lb. ($\frac{1}{2}$ kg.), for 30 minutes for 1–1$\frac{1}{2}$ lb. ($\frac{1}{2}$–$\frac{3}{4}$ kg.), and for over 2 lb. (1 kg.) 45 minutes. Cool in the liquid and drain well.

3. Split the lobster down the centre, remove the dark intestinal vein which runs up the side of the body and the stomach at the top. Break the large claws, flake the meat and either arrange this on the salad or on top of the body of the halved lobster.

4. Break the tiny claws away from the lobster body and arrange these, as shown in the picture, as a garnish.

5. Slice the cucumber and tomato thinly. Arrange on the lobster. Serve chilled, on a bed of lettuce and watercress, with mayonnaise.

Variation

The lobster meat may be removed from the shell and piled neatly on the bed of salad.

Salmon mousse

Cooking time: 12 minutes
Preparation time: 25 minutes
Main cooking utensils: saucepan, 5-inch (13-cm.) soufflé dish,
   greaseproof paper
Serves: 6–8

Imperial	**Metric**
1¼ oz. margarine	35 g. margarine
1 oz. flour	25 g. flour
½ pint milk	250 ml. milk
seasoning	seasoning
1 tablespoon lemon juice	1 tablespoon lemon juice
½ oz. powdered gelatine	15 g. powdered gelatine
4 tablespoons water	4 tablespoons water
1 lb. canned or cooked salmon	½ kg. canned or cooked salmon
few drops anchovy essence	few drops anchovy essence
2 medium-sized ripe tomatoes	2 medium-sized ripe tomatoes
¼ pint double cream	125 ml. double cream
2 egg whites	2 egg whites
To garnish:	*To garnish:*
1–2 stuffed olives	1–2 stuffed olives
1 small gherkin	1 small gherkin
6 wafer-thin slices cucumber	6 wafer-thin slices cucumber

1. Tie a double band of greaseproof paper around the outside of the soufflé dish, grease lightly with the ¼ oz. (10 g.) margarine.

2. Make the white sauce with 1 oz. (25 g.) margarine, the flour, milk and seasoning. Add lemon juice.

3. Dissolve the gelatine in hot water, add to the sauce, allow to cool, covering with damp paper to prevent a skin forming.

4. Stir in the flaked salmon, anchovy essence and tomato purée (made by rubbing tomatoes through a sieve).

5. Allow the mixture to stiffen slightly, then fold in lightly whipped cream and the stiffly beaten egg whites.

6. Put into the soufflé dish, allow to set, then carefully remove paper.

7. Garnish with small pieces of stuffed olive, gherkin, and slices of cucumber.

8. Serve with mayonnaise, well flavoured with lemon juice and with a potato salad made by mixing cooked diced potato with mayonnaise, chopped spring onions or grated onion, and garnish with tomato, cucumber skin or parsley.

Sole véronique

Cooking time: 25–30 minutes
Preparation time: 20 minutes
Main cooking utensils: ovenproof dish, saucepan
Oven temperature: moderate (350–375°F., 180–190°C., Gas
   Mark 4–5)
Oven position: centre
Serves: 4

Imperial	Metric
4 large or 8 small fillets sole	4 large or 8 small fillets sole
6 oz. white grapes	150 g. white grapes
seasoning	seasoning
$\frac{1}{2}$ pint white wine, or half wine and half milk	250 ml. white wine, or half wine and half milk
1 oz. butter	25 g. butter
1 oz. flour	25 g. flour
2–3 tablespoons cream	2–3 tablespoons cream
2 egg yolks (optional)	2 egg yolks (optional)
To garnish:	*To garnish:*
few extra grapes	few extra grapes
parsley	parsley

1. Skin the fillets; skin and pip the grapes.
2. Place some of the grapes on the fillets, fold over; season lightly.
3. Put into the buttered dish, add white wine and cook for approximately 15 minutes.
4. Lift the fillets of fish carefully from the liquid, save this to add to the sauce.
5. To make the sauce, heat the butter, stir in the flour, cook for 2–3 minutes, then blend in the strained wine (or use the wine and add milk to give good $\frac{1}{2}$ pint (250 ml)), bring to the boil, cook until thickened.
6. When smooth and thickened, add cream beaten with the egg yolks, and cook gently, without boiling for 2–3 minutes.
7. Season well, and pour over the fish.
8. Garnish with a few extra grapes and parsley, and serve with a green salad.

Variation

The grapes can be added to the sauce to heat. Skinned and deseeded black grapes can be used (do not skin the grapes if you want them to give a good colour in the garnish).

Steak en croûte

Cooking time: 40 minutes onwards, see stages 4, 5
Preparation time: 25 minutes
Main cooking utensil: baking tray or sheet
Oven temperature: hot (425–450°F., 220–230°C., Gas Mark 7–8)
   then moderate to moderately hot (350–375°F., 180–190°C.,
   Gas Mark 4–5)
Oven position: centre
Serves: 4–6

Imperial	Metric
Shortcrust pastry:	*Shortcrust pastry:*
7 oz. flour	175 g. flour
pinch salt	pinch salt
3½ oz. fat	90 g. fat
water to mix	water to mix
Filling:	*Filling:*
3 oz. mushrooms	75 g. mushrooms
2 oz. butter	50 g. butter
seasoning	seasoning
1–1½ lb. fillet or rump steak	½–¾ kg. fillet or rump steak
(cut in one piece)	(cut in one piece)

1. Sieve the flour and salt, rub in the fat, then bind with water, roll out to a long oblong piece.

2. Blend the finely chopped mushrooms with the butter and seasoning, spread over the centre of the pastry leaving ends plain.

3. Put the steak on top, season lightly and wrap the pastry around this, sealing the edges with water.

4. Cook on the lightly greased baking tray for 20–25 minutes.

5. Lower heat as given and allow extra 20 minutes for under done steak; 25–30 minutes for medium cooked steak; 35–40 minutes for well done.

6. Serve with vegetables, or a green salad.

Variation

Mix ¾–1 lb. (350–450 g.) beef or pork sausage meat (or use half minced beef, and half sausage meat) with a diced green and diced red pepper; add 1–2 chopped apples. Fry 2 chopped onions in 1 oz. (25 g.) fat, stir into the mixture, bind with 2 eggs and season well. Form into a loaf and use instead of fillet or rump steak.

La daube provençale

Cooking time: 4 hours
Preparation time: 30 minutes plus time for beef to marinate
Main cooking utensil: large casserole
Oven temperature: cool (275–300°F., 140–150°C., Gas Mark 1–2)
Oven position: centre
Serves: 6–8

Imperial	Metric
2 lb. stewing beef	1 kg. stewing beef
$\frac{1}{2}$ pint white wine	250 ml. white wine
1 tablespoon chopped parsley	1 tablespoon chopped parsley
$\frac{1}{2}$ tablespoon chopped thyme	$\frac{1}{2}$ tablespoon chopped thyme
1 bay leaf	1 bay leaf
1 tablespoon oil	1 tablespoon oil
6 rashers bacon	6 rashers bacon
2 large carrots	2 large carrots
1 large onion	1 large onion
seasoning	seasoning
2–4 oz. mushrooms	50–100 g. mushrooms
8 oz. tomatoes	200 g. tomatoes
1 clove garlic	1 clove garlic
few stoned olives	few stoned olives
$\frac{1}{2}$ pint brown stock or water and a stock cube	250 ml. brown stock or water and a stock cube

1. Cut the meat into 1-inch (2·5 cm.) cubes.

2. Make a marinade with the white wine, herbs and oil.

3. Put the beef in this, allow to stand in a cool place for 3 hours.

4. After this time, remove the bacon rinds from the bacon, place these in the bottom of the casserole with the sliced carrots, sliced onion and seasoning.

5. Add the sliced mushrooms and chopped tomatoes.

6. Lift the beef from the marinade, put over the vegetable base, sprinkle with the crushed clove of garlic and seasoning.

7. Cover with the diced bacon and olives.

8. Blend the wine and herbs with the stock, pour into the casserole.

9. Cover the casserole and cook until tender.

10. Serve with a green salad or with mixed vegetables.

Variation

Use red wine instead of white. Thicken the liquid if liked.

Beef stroganoff

Cooking time: 25 minutes
Preparation time: 15 minutes
Main cooking utensil: large covered saucepan
Serves: 4–5

Imperial

1¼–1½ lb. fillet of beef
seasoning
2 small onions
3 oz. butter
3–4 oz. mushrooms
¼ pint smetana (soured cream,
    see note)
1 dessertspoon flour
pinch mustard
little extra smetana
To garnish:
parsley

Metric

about ¾ kg. fillet of beef
seasoning
2 small onions
75 g. butter
75–100 g. mushrooms
125 ml. smetana (soured cream,
    see note)
1 dessertspoon flour
pinch mustard
little extra smetana
To garnish:
parsley

1. Cut the meat into thin strips 2 inches (5 cm.) long and season.

2. Fry the chopped onion in hot butter until golden coloured.

3. Add the sliced mushrooms to the onions and add the meat and fry for 5 minutes.

4. Blend the smetana with the flour and mustard and pour into the pan.

5. Stir well, cover the pan, simmer gently for 10 minutes until the meat is tender.

6. Add more smetana before serving with rice or creamed potatoes and a green salad. Garnish with parsley.

Note: If smetana is not available use fresh cream soured with 1 tablespoon lemon juice.

Variations

2 tablespoons brandy can be added to the sauce at stage 6.
1 tablespoon tomato purée can be added at stage 4.

Economical beef stroganoff: Use stewing steak. Fry in hot butter with mushrooms, then add packet onion soup blended with 1 pint (scant ½ litre) water. Simmer for 1¼–1½ hours then proceed as stage 4, using soured cream or natural yoghurt.

Beef bourguignonne

Cooking time: meat — few minutes, sauces — 5–10 minutes
Preparation time: 30 minutes
Main cooking utensils: fondue pan, fondue heater, fondue forks
Serves: 4

Imperial	Metric
allow 4–6 oz. fillet or rump steak per person	allow 100–150 g. fillet or rump steak per person
corn oil for deep frying	corn oil for deep frying
Savoury sauce tartare:	*Savoury sauce tartare:*
2 tomatoes	2 tomatoes
2 hard-boiled eggs	2 hard-boiled eggs
1 small onion	1 small onion
1 tablespoon capers	1 tablespoon capers
2–3 gherkins	2–3 gherkins
$\frac{1}{2}$ pint mayonnaise	250 ml. mayonnaise
Creamy tomato mayonnaise:	*Creamy tomato mayonnaise:*
white sauce made with 1 oz. butter, 1 oz. flour, $\frac{1}{2}$ pint milk, or packet white sauce mix and $\frac{1}{2}$ pint milk	white sauce made with 25 g. butter, 25 g. flour, 250 ml. milk, or packet white sauce mix and 250 ml. milk
2 tablespoons tomato purée	2 tablespoons tomato purée
$\frac{1}{2}$ pint mayonnaise	250 ml. mayonnaise
Curry mayonnaise:	*Curry mayonnaise:*
white sauce as above	white sauce as above
1 dessertspoon curry paste	1 dessertspoon curry paste
$\frac{1}{2}$ pint mayonnaise	250 ml. mayonnaise

This is an ideal celebration dish which guests can cook freshly as needed.

1. Cut meat into $\frac{1}{2}$-$\frac{3}{4}$-inch (1–1$\frac{1}{2}$-cm.) cubes.
2. Fill the pan one-third full with corn oil, heat to 375°F. (190°C.), remove from cooker, place over fondue heater so the oil does not become too hot.
3. Let each guest spear pieces of meat on to fondue forks and fry in the hot corn oil for 1–5 minutes depending on personal taste, then dip into the sauces.
4. To make savoury sauce tartare, skin the tomatoes and chop with all the other ingredients; add to the mayonnaise.
5. For the creamy tomato mayonnaise, make 1 pint (500 ml.) white sauce. Use half for this dip, blending it with the tomato purée and mayonnaise.
6. For the curry mayonnaise, use the remainder of the white sauce but cook for 1–2 minutes with the curry paste, cool and add to mayonnaise.
7. Put the fondue pan in the middle of the table with dips arrayed around it and serve with crusty French bread, rolls, or savoury biscuits.

Mawarra meat curry

Cooking time: 3 hours
Preparation time: 30 minutes
Main cooking utensils: saucepan, casserole
Oven temperature: moderate (350°F., 180°C., Gas Mark 4)
Oven position: centre
Serves: 4–5

Imperial	Metric
1¼ lb. chuck steak	600 g. chuck steak
1 oz. fat	25 g. fat
1 large onion	1 large onion
1–2 level tablespoons curry powder	1–2 level tablespoons curry powder
1 level tablespoon paprika pepper	1 level tablespoon paprika pepper
2 oz. walnuts	50 g. walnuts
2 oz. blanched almonds	50 g. blanched almonds
1 oz. flour	25 g. flour
¾ pint stock	375 ml. stock
seasoning	seasoning
2 oz. desiccated coconut	50 g. desiccated coconut
2 oz. sultanas	50 g. sultanas
1 level tablespoon redcurrant jelly	1 level tablespoon redcurrant jelly
1 tablespoon lemon juice	1 tablespoon lemon juice
To serve:	*To serve:*
8 oz. rice, boiled (see note)	200 g. rice, boiled (see note)

1. Cut the meat into neat dice.
2. Melt the fat and fry the meat and chopped onion until beginning to brown.
3. Add the curry powder, paprika, chopped walnuts and almonds and continue to cook for 3 minutes.
4. Stir in the flour, cook gently for several minutes.
5. Gradually blend in the stock, bring to the boil and cook until thickened.
6. Season and add the coconut, sultanas, redcurrant jelly and lemon juice.
7. Transfer to a casserole, cover and cook in the oven.
8. Arrange the curry in a dish and surround with a border of cooked rice. Serve with curry accompaniments.

Note: To boil rice, allow 3 pints (1½ litres) boiling water. Put in the rice, cook until tender. Drain and rinse in boiling water, or cold water and reheat.

Variation
Use less curry powder and paprika pepper for a milder flavour.

Treacle-glazed gammon

Cooking time: 2½ hours
Preparation time: few minutes, plus overnight soaking
Main cooking utensils: large saucepan, roasting tin
Oven temperature: moderate to moderately hot (350–375°F.,
   180–190°C., Gas Mark 4–5)
Oven position: centre
Serves: 8–10

Imperial	Metric
5 lb. middle gammon	2½ kg. middle gammon
4 tablespoons black treacle	4 tablespoons black treacle
12 peppercorns	12 peppercorns
1 bay leaf	1 bay leaf
cloves	cloves
¼ pint dry cider	125 ml. dry cider

1. Soak the gammon overnight, rinse in cold running water, place in a saucepan and cover with cold water.
2. Add 2 tablespoons black treacle, the peppercorns and the bay leaf; bring slowly to the boil and simmer gently for 1½ hours.
3. Drain the joint, strip off the skin and score the fat into diamonds with a sharp knife. Insert a clove in each diamond.
4. Warm the remaining 2 tablespoons of black treacle and pour over the fat surface. Place the joint in a roasting tin and pour the cider over the top.
5. Cook for approximately 1 hour basting frequently with the cider.
6. Serve hot with vegetables, or cold on a bed of lettuce.

Note: Store the gammon in the refrigerator. It is delicious cold.

Variation
Use half treacle and half golden syrup or honey.

Moussaka

Cooking time: 2–2½ hours
Preparation time: 35 minutes
Main cooking utensils: large frying pan, covered casserole
Oven temperature: very moderate (325–350°F., 170–180°C., Gas Mark 3–4)
Oven position: centre
Serves: 4–6

Imperial	Metric
3 oz. butter	75 g. butter
8 oz. onions	200 g. onions
2 large aubergines (see note)	2 large aubergines (see note)
1–1½ lb. potatoes	½–¾ kg. potatoes
Sauce:	*Sauce:*
1 oz. butter	25 g. butter
1 oz. flour	25 g. flour
½ pint milk	250 ml. milk
seasoning	seasoning
2–3 oz. cheese	50–75 g. cheese
1 egg	1 egg
1 lb. minced meat (see variation)	½ kg. minced meat (see variation)
2–4 tomatoes	2–4 tomatoes
To garnish:	*To garnish:*
parsley	parsley

1. Heat the butter and fry the sliced onions until tender but not broken.

2. Remove the onions from the butter, then fry sliced aubergines and thinly sliced potatoes turning until well coated.

3. Make the sauce, heat the butter, then add the flour and cook for several minutes, remove from the heat, then gradually add the milk, stirring.

4. Bring to the boil and cook, stirring, until thickened and smooth; add seasoning and the grated cheese and beaten egg – do not cook again.

5. Arrange a layer of the aubergine mixture in the dish, top with the well-seasoned meat, onion, and sliced tomato.

6. Put a small amount of sauce on each layer and continue filling the dish ending with a layer of sauce.

7. Cover with lid and cook for 1½ hours. (Remove the lid for the last 30 minutes, to allow the top to brown.)

8. Serve garnished with parsley.

Note : Aubergines are often called eggplants. They do not need peeling.

Variation

In Turkey and the Balkan countries lamb and mutton are used due to availability, but minced beef or pork could be used.

Crown roast of lamb

Cooking time: see stage 8
Preparation time: 20 minutes
Main cooking utensils: saucepan, roasting tin
Oven temperature: moderately hot (375–400°F., 190–200°C.,
   Gas Mark 5–6)
Oven position: centre
Serves: 6–14 (depending on the size of the chops)

Imperial	Metric
1 or 2 joints of loin, approximately 12–14 chops	1 or 2 joints of loin, approximately 12–14 chops
1 oz. butter or fat	25 g. butter or fat
seasoning	seasoning
Prune and apricot stuffing:	*Prune and apricot stuffing:*
1 oz. butter	25 g. butter
1 medium onion, chopped	1 medium onion, chopped
2 oz. boiled rice	50 g. boiled rice
4 oz. prunes, chopped and stoned	100 g. prunes, chopped and stoned
1 oz. ground almonds	25 g. ground almonds
3–4 whole apricots, fresh or canned	3–4 whole apricots, fresh or canned
1 tablespoon chopped parsley	1 tablespoon chopped parsley
grated rind of 1 lemon	grated rind of 1 lemon
juice of 1 lemon	juice of 1 lemon
1 egg	1 egg
seasoning	seasoning

1. Ask the butcher to cut and tie the meat into a round (crown roast), brush with melted butter or fat and season.

2. Melt the butter and cook the chopped onion until transparent.

3. Add the rice and prunes and cook together for a few minutes.

4. Mix in ground almonds, sliced apricots, parsley, lemon rind and juice.

5. Bind with egg and season.

6. Place the stuffing in the centre of the crown roast.

7. Wrap a piece of kitchen foil around each bone to protect it while cooking.

8. Roast for 25 minutes to the lb. ($\frac{1}{2}$ kg.) and 25 minutes over, weighing the roast after stuffing.

9. Remove the foil and place a cutlet frill on the end of each bone.

Note: Keep in the refrigerator, as it can be served cold.

Variation

Roast the meat in the usual way, without the stuffing. Fill the crown with cooked vegetables.

Shish kebabs

Cooking time: 10–15 minutes
Preparation time: 10 minutes
Main cooking utensils: four metal skewers, grill pan
Serves: 4

Imperial	Metric
approximately 1 lb. lamb, cut from top of leg	approximately $\frac{1}{2}$ kg. lamb, cut from top of leg
8 oz. chipolata sausages	200 g. chipolata sausages
4 oz. large mushrooms	100 g. large mushrooms
1 green pepper	1 green pepper
seasoning	seasoning
2 oz. butter, melted	50 g. butter, melted
To garnish:	*To garnish:*
canned corn and pepper	canned corn and pepper

1. Divide the meat into 1-inch (2·5-cm.) cubes.

2. Prick the sausages and cut the stalks from the mushrooms and slice the green pepper, discarding the core and seeds.

3. Put the ingredients on to the metal skewers, seasoning lightly.

4. Brush with melted butter, and put under a hot grill.

5. Cook until the meat is tender, turning several times and brushing liberally with melted butter.

6. Heat the corn, drain and put on to a hot serving dish, top with the kebabs.

7. Serve with a green salad.

Variations

Other ingredients may be added: halved skinned lamb's kidneys, small parboiled onions, small firm tomatoes, aubergine slices. Steak can be used in place of lamb. Arrange the kebabs on a bed of cooked rice instead of corn.

Sweet and sour pork

Cooking time: 6 minutes
Preparation time: 35 minutes
Main cooking utensils: saucepan, pan for oil
Serves: 3–4

Imperial	**Metric**
Batter:	*Batter:*
3 oz. flour (with plain flour use $\frac{1}{2}$ teaspoon baking powder)	75 g. flour (with plain flour use $\frac{1}{2}$ teaspoon baking powder)
$\frac{1}{2}$ small egg	$\frac{1}{2}$ small egg
$\frac{1}{4}$ pint water	125 ml. water
$\frac{1}{2}$ teaspoon oil	$\frac{1}{2}$ teaspoon oil
Vegetables:	*Vegetables:*
1 tablespoon each of pickled cabbage, cucumber, carrot, salt, vinegar	1 tablespoon each of pickled cabbage, cucumber, carrot, salt, vinegar
6 oz. leg of pork	150 g. leg of pork
seasoning (see note)	seasoning (see note)
$\frac{1}{2}$ teaspoon oil	$\frac{1}{2}$ teaspoon oil
$\frac{1}{2}$ teaspoon sherry	$\frac{1}{2}$ teaspoon sherry
1 tablespoon flour	1 tablespoon flour
oil for frying	oil for frying
Sweet-sour sauce:	*Sweet-sour sauce:*
$\frac{3}{4}$ teaspoon cornflour	$\frac{3}{4}$ teaspoon cornflour
7 tablespoons water	7 tablespoons water
1 dessertspoon sugar	1 dessertspoon sugar
seasoning	seasoning
$\frac{1}{2}$ teaspoon soy sauce	$\frac{1}{2}$ teaspoon soy sauce
$\frac{1}{2}$ teaspoon tomato ketchup	$\frac{1}{2}$ teaspoon tomato ketchup

1. To make the batter, sieve the flour, add the egg, water and oil, beat until smooth.

2. Cut the vegetables into thin matchsticks, sprinkle with the salt and allow to stand 5 minutes; press out the liquid, sprinkle with a little more salt and vinegar.

3. Cut the pork into 1-inch (2·5-cm.) cubes add seasoning, oil and sherry, work well into the meat, then coat with the flour.

4. Put into a sieve to shake off the surplus flour.

5. To make the sauce, blend the cornflour with half the water, put into a pan with the rest of the ingredients and remaining water, bring to the boil, stir well, keep hot.

6. Heat the oil and fry the pork in this for a few minutes until golden brown.

7. Drain on absorbent paper.

8. Serve the pork in a hot dish. Add the vegetables and spoon over the sweet-sour sauce.

Note : If possible include a pinch of monosodium glutamate.

Chicken chaudfroid salad

Cooking time: few minutes to heat water for aspic jelly
Preparation time: 20 minutes and time for sauce to stand
Main utensils: palette knife and pastry brush, wire cooling tray
Serves: 4

Imperial	Metric
4 joints cooked chicken	4 joints cooked chicken
Chaudfroid sauce:	*Chaudfroid sauce:*
½ envelope aspic jelly powder (see note)	½ envelope aspic jelly powder (see note)
1 teaspoon powdered gelatine	1 teaspoon powdered gelatine
¼ pint very hot water	125 ml. very hot water
¼ pint mayonnaise	125 ml. mayonnaise
To garnish:	*To garnish:*
tomato	tomato
cucumber	cucumber
watercress	watercress

1. Trim away the skin from the chicken, and remove the bones if using leg joints.

2. Blend the aspic jelly powder and powdered gelatine and dissolve thoroughly in the hot water.

3. Cool slightly, then stir into the mayonnaise and allow to begin to thicken very slightly.

4. Stand the chicken on the wire cooling tray with a plate or tray underneath.

5. Spread or brush the half set sauce over the chicken until it is completely coated, any drips should be scraped up and used.

6. Leave to set, then remove from the wire cooling tray.

7. Arrange on a serving dish and garnish with sliced tomato, cucumber and watercress.

Note: Most envelopes of aspic jelly contain enough to set ½ pint (250 ml.) liquid.

Variations

Instead of mayonnaise a very well-flavoured white sauce can be used. Instead of aspic jelly use well-seasoned chicken stock and 2½ teaspoons powdered gelatine. Cooked salmon can be coated in the same way, in which case use fish stock instead of water.

Chicken casserole bonne femme

Cooking time: $2\frac{1}{4}$–$2\frac{1}{2}$ hours
Preparation time: 30 minutes
Main cooking utensil: large suacepan
Serves: 6–8

Imperial	Metric
chicken liver	chicken liver
8 oz. pork sausage meat	200 g. pork sausage meat
mixed herbs	mixed herbs
1 boiling fowl	1 boiling fowl
1 oz. butter	25 g. butter
1 tablespoon oil	1 tablespoon oil
little diced celery	little diced celery
few celery leaves	few celery leaves
2 turnips, diced	2 turnips, diced
6 carrots	6 carrots
seasoning	seasoning
2 bay leaves	2 bay leaves
sprig sage or pinch dried herbs	sprig sage or pinch dried herbs
sprig thyme or pinch dried thyme	sprig thyme or pinch dried thyme
4–6 potatoes	4–6 potatoes
little cream (optional)	little cream (optional)

1. Blend the diced raw chicken liver with the sausage meat and herbs and put this into chicken, tying or skewering firmly.
2. Heat the chicken in butter and oil until golden.
3. Add all the rest of the ingredients (tying the herbs in a bouquet garni, if liked), except the potatoes and cream.
4. Cover the pan tightly and simmer gently for 1½ hours.
5. Add finely diced potatoes and continue cooking for a further 30–45 minutes.
6. Lift the chicken on to a dish with the whole vegetables.
7. Remove the herbs and beat the potatoes into the stock to make a thickened sauce, adding a little cream and extra seasoning if required.

Variations
Add a little diced bacon fat, mushrooms, onions or other vegetables. Use a roasting chicken and cook for 45 minutes at stage 4.

Roast turkey

Cooking time: see stages 3, 4 and 5
Preparation time: 20 minutes
Oven temperature: hot (425–450°F., 220–230°C., Gas Mark 7–8)
Serves: 8–12

Imperial	Metric
10-lb. turkey (see note)	5-kg. turkey (see note)
Stuffing:	*Stuffing:*
8 oz. fresh white breadcrumbs	200 g. fresh white breadcrumbs
4 oz. shredded suet	100 g. shredded suet
2 teaspoons chopped parsley	2 teaspoons chopped parsley
1 teaspoon mixed dried herbs or lemon thyme	1 teaspoon mixed dried herbs or lemon thyme
2 teaspoons lemon juice	2 teaspoons lemon juice
2 eggs, beaten	2 eggs, beaten
seasoning	seasoning
To prepare for roasting:	*To prepare for roasting:*
cover the turkey generously with butter or clarified fat to prevent drying	cover the turkey generously with butter or clarified fat to prevent drying

1. Make the stuffing by mixing all the ingredients together. Do not make this too dry.

2. Put it into the neck end of the bird.

3. Weigh the bird after stuffing, cooking time depends on this.

4. Allow 15 minutes cooking time per lb. ($\frac{1}{2}$ kg.) and 15 minutes over up to 12 lb. (6 kg.) For each additional lb. ($\frac{1}{2}$ kg.) over 12 lb. (6 kg.) allow extra 12 minutes cooking time.

5. If cooking in a covered roaster or foil, allow an extra 20 minutes cooking time or use a very hot oven.

6. If using foil, open this for the last 45 minutes of the cooking time to allow turkey to brown.

7. With an open roasting tin, baste once or twice during cooking.

8. Serve with stuffing, small sausages and bacon rolls; put sausages into the tin with the turkey 30 minutes before the end of the cooking time. For the bacon rolls, roll pieces of bacon on skewers and place around the turkey 15–20 minutes before the end of the cooking time.

Note : Frozen turkey should be thoroughly defrosted before cooking; allow up to 48 hours for this. The bones of the turkey weigh heavily, so allow 1 lb. ($\frac{1}{2}$ kg.) uncooked per person.

Duck nantaise

Cooking time: see stage 1
Preparation time: 10 minutes
Main cooking utensil: roasting tin
Oven temperature: hot (425–450°F., 220–230°C., Gas Mark 7–8)
Oven position: above centre
Serves: 4

Imperial	Metric
1 oven-ready duck, about 4½ lb.	1 oven-ready duck, about 2¼ kg.
4–6 oz. fairly lean bacon	100–150 g. fairly lean bacon
3–4 medium-sized onions, cooked for 15–20 minutes in salted water	3–4 medium-sized onions, cooked for 15–20 minutes in salted water

1. Weigh the duck and allow to cook for 15 minutes per lb. (½ kg.) and 15 minutes over.

2. After the duck has been cooking for approximately 30 minutes, prick the skin gently with a fine skewer to allow surplus fat to run out, and add the chopped rashers of bacon and the quartered onions. Toss in the duck fat and continue cooking.

3. Place the duck on a dish and garnish with cooked peas, pieces of onion and bacon.

4. Serve with thickened gravy made as follows: make a stock by simmering the giblets. Pour away the fat from the roasting tin, leaving 1 tablespoon. Blend in 1 oz. (25 g.) flour, gravy flavouring, seasoning and ½ pint (250 ml.) stock. Bring to the boil, stirring, and simmer for 1–2 minutes.

Note: This is the name given in France to a duckling from the Nantaise area; in this particular recipe the duck has an interesting garnish, but has not been stuffed. To carve large ducks, divide into 4 portions — 2 breasts and wings, and 2 legs. Divide smaller ducks, down the centre, into 2 portions.

Variation

Use new young parboiled baby turnips in place of the onions.

Hawaiian duck with bananas

Cooking time: just over 1 hour
Preparation time: 30 minutes
Main cooking utensils: roasting tin, ovenproof dish, saucepan
Oven temperature: moderate to moderately hot (400°F., 200°C.,
  Gas Mark 6)
Oven position: centre and near top
Serves: 4

Imperial	Metric
1 young duckling	1 young duckling
little oil	little oil
1 medium-sized can pineapple	1 medium-sized can pineapple
$\frac{1}{2}$ pint red wine	250 ml. red wine
seasoning	seasoning
4 bananas	4 bananas
juice of $\frac{1}{2}$ lemon	juice of $\frac{1}{2}$ lemon
Pineapple sauce:	*Pineapple sauce:*
$\frac{1}{2}$ oz. cornflour	15 g. cornflour
1 orange	1 orange
liquid from roasting tin	liquid from roasting tin
To garnish:	*To garnish:*
parsley	parsley

1. Cut the duckling into neat joints and put these into the tin.

2. Brush well with the oil.

3. Pour the syrup from the can of pineapple and the wine over the duck.

4. Add seasoning, cook for approximately 40 minutes, until the duck is quite tender.

5. Baste with the pineapple and wine frequently, so the flavour impregnates the flesh of the duck.

6. Put the unpeeled bananas in an ovenproof dish, brush skins with oil.

7. Sprinkle with lemon juice and bake towards the top of the oven for 10 minutes.

8. To make the sauce, blend the cornflour with the orange juice. Put into a pan with the liquid from the roasting tin (made up to $\frac{1}{2}$ pint (250 ml.) with water). Bring to the boil and cook until thickened and smooth, adding grated orange rind and most of the chopped canned pineapple.

9. Place the duck on a dish, arrange the bananas around. Garnish with the remaining pineapple and the parsley.

10. Serve with boiled, mashed sweet potatoes.

Pizza

Cooking time: 25–30 minutes
Preparation time: 35 minutes plus time for proving
Main cooking utensils: large baking tray, saucepan
Oven temperature: hot (425–450°F., 220–230°C., Gas Mark 7–8)
Serves: 6–8

Imperial	Metric
Dough:	*Dough:*
8 oz. plain flour	200 g. plain flour
1 level teaspoon salt	1 level teaspoon salt
½ oz. yeast	15 g. yeast
¼ pint lukewarm milk	125 ml. lukewarm milk
1 small egg	1 small egg
1 oz. butter or margarine	25 g. butter or margarine
Topping:	*Topping:*
½ oz. vegetable cooking fat or 1 tablespoon oil	15 g. vegetable cooking fat or 1 tablespoon oil
1 small onion	1 small onion
8 oz. tomatoes	200 g. tomatoes
2½-oz. can tomato purée	65-g. can tomato purée
1 teaspoon sugar	1 teaspoon sugar
seasoning	seasoning
1 bay leaf	1 bay leaf
pinch oregano	pinch oregano
1 small can anchovy fillets	1 small can anchovy fillets
1 oz. cheese	25 g. cheese
4–6 olives	4–6 olives

1. For the dough, sieve the flour and salt.

2. Cream the yeast with a little warm milk, add the egg and the rest of the milk.

3. Add gradually to the flour, blend in softened, but not melted, butter.

4. Beat well with the hand until mixture comes away from one's fingers; return to the bowl.

5. Cover with a cloth, leave to prove for 40 minutes in a warm place.

6. Melt the fat, fry the chopped onion until tender and golden.

7. Add the tomatoes, (use canned tomatoes, or fresh skinned tomatoes with 2 tablespoons water), tomato purée, sugar, seasoning, bay leaf and oregano.

8. Simmer for 10–15 minutes, until the mixture thickens. Cool.

9. Grease the baking tray.

10. Pat out dough with hands to a 9-inch (23-cm.) round. Cover to within ½ inch (1 cm.) of the edge with the filling.

11. Garnish with thinly sliced anchovies, grated cheese and olives.

12. Prove in warm place for 15 minutes.

13. Bake in the centre of the oven for the time given.

14. Serve hot or cold.

Variation

Add tuna or sardines at stage 8.

Mediterranean rice

Cooking time: 45–50 minutes
Preparation time: 15 minutes
Main cooking utensil: large saucepan
Serves: 4

Imperial	Metric
1 small chicken	1 small chicken
2–3 tablespoons oil	2–3 tablespoons oil
3 medium-sized green peppers	3 medium-sized green peppers
8 oz. tomatoes	200 g. tomatoes
1 clove garlic	1 clove garlic
8 oz. long-grain rice	200 g. long-grain rice
7-oz. can tuna fish	175-g. can tuna fish
3-oz. can shrimps	75-g. can shrimps
8 oz. green peas, fresh or frozen	200 g. green peas, fresh or frozen
1 pint stock or water	generous $\frac{1}{2}$ litre stock or water

1. Cut the chicken into small joints and fry in a heavy pan in oil until golden brown.

2. Shred the green peppers, discarding cores and seeds.

3. Add to the chicken with the sliced tomatoes, crushed garlic and rice.

4. Fry gently for 5 minutes, stirring well.

5. Add the drained, flaked tuna fish, shrimps, peas and stock.

6. Cook over a gentle heat for approximately 30–40 minutes, until chicken and rice are cooked, and the liquid just absorbed.

7. Serve with a green salad.

Variation

Omit the tuna and shrimps and add chopped mushrooms. Can be served cold. Cook as above, while hot toss in a little oil and lemon juice.

Persian pilaff

Cooking time: 45 minutes
Preparation time: 25 minutes
Main cooking utensil: strong covered saucepan
Serves: 6

Imperial
3 oz. chicken fat
10–12 chicken livers
8 oz. carrots
2 medium onions
small bunch parsley
10 oz. long- or medium-grain
  rice
1¾ pints chicken stock or water
1½ teaspoons turmeric
seasoning
little crushed garlic or garlic
  salt (optional)
2 large tomatoes

Metric
75 g. chicken fat
10–12 chicken livers
200 g. carrots
2 medium onions
small bunch parsley
250 g. long- or medium-grain
  rice
1 litre chicken stock or water
1½ teaspoons turmeric
seasoning
little crushed garlic or garlic
  salt (optional)
2 large tomatoes

1. Heat the chicken fat in the saucepan. Then add the chicken livers and fry lightly.

2. Cut into neat pieces — they keep more moist if treated this way.

3. Grate the carrots, chop the onions and parsley.

4. Add to the chicken fat remaining in the pan and fry for 5 minutes, taking care the onion does not brown.

5. Add the liver and the rest of the ingredients, except tomatoes, to the pan.

6. Cover the pan tightly and cook, without stirring, over a low heat for approximately 30 minutes until the rice has absorbed the liquid — it should not become too dry.

7. Chop the tomatoes neatly — skin if wished, then add to the rice mixture.

8. Serve as a light lunch dish.

Variation

Omit the turmeric (this gives the rice colour as well as a delicate flavour) and add more or less vegetables to taste.

Turkish stuffed vine leaves

Cooking time: 1 hour
Preparation time: 20 minutes
Main cooking utensil: large saucepan
Serves: 6

Imperial	Metric
1 large onion	1 large onion
3 tablespoons olive oil	3 tablespoons olive oil
6 tablespoons raw rice	6 tablespoons raw rice
4 tablespoons pine nuts or shredded almonds	4 tablespoons pine nuts or shredded almonds
12 oz. raw minced beef	300 g. raw minced beef
pinch fresh chopped mint or dried mint	pinch fresh chopped mint or dried mint
seasoning	seasoning
pinch cinnamon	pinch cinnamon
approximately 30 young vine leaves	approximately 30 young vine leaves
$\frac{1}{4}$ pint wine, preferably a dry white wine	125 ml. wine, preferably a dry white wine

1. Chop the onion and fry in the hot oil for a few minutes, then add the rice and fry gently until pale golden.

2. Add the pine nuts and cook for 1 minute.

3. Remove from the heat, add the meat, mint, seasoning and cinnamon; mix well.

4. Dip the vine leaves for 1 minute in hot water to tenderise them. Remove with a perforated spoon.

5. Spread the vine leaves out flat, and put 1 tablespoon of the meat mixture in the centre of each.

6. Fold in the ends, and roll into finger shapes.

7. Put rolls into a pan, cover with the wine, add water if necessary to cover the leaves, for they must not be left dry at the beginning.

8. Cook for approximately 25 minutes over a low heat, then remove lid so the liquid gradually evaporates.

9. These are generally served as an hors d'oeuvre and can be served hot or cold. Garnish with any extra filling.

Variation

Use all water or stock and lemon juice in place of the wine.

Fresh fruit salad

Cooking time: few minutes for syrup
Preparation time: 10–20 minutes depending on fruit used
Main cooking utensil: saucepan
Serves: 4

Imperial	Metric
1—2 oranges	1—2 oranges
$\frac{1}{4}$ pint water	125 ml. water
2 oz. sugar	50 g. sugar
1—2 apples	1—2 apples
1—2 pears	1—2 pears
few grapes and/or cherries	few grapes and/or cherries
2 small bananas	2 small bananas

1. Peel the oranges. The best way to do this for a fruit salad is to cut away the peel and remove the white pith at the same time. Cut the orange into segments between the skin, discard any pips.
2. To have a good flavoured syrup, boil the peel with the water and sugar for 5 minutes only.
3. Slice the apples and pears — the peel may be left on bright coloured apples if required.
4. Pip grapes, stone cherries. The easiest way to do this is with a very fine hairpin (see note).
5. Slice peeled bananas.
6. Put into the serving dish, cover with the syrup.
7. Serve chilled.

Note: The tip of a hairpin or a fine hatpin can be inserted into grapes to pull out the stones without breaking the fruit. The bent end should be inserted into cherries, hooked around the stone and just pulled out gently but firmly. Store the salad in the refrigerator. The flavour of a fruit salad is improved if it is left for a few hours.

Variation

Other fruits can be added when in season. The syrup can be replaced by fresh orange juice or a little white wine or Kirsch.

Pineapple fruit salad

Cooking time: few minutes
Preparation time: 15 minutes
Main cooking utensil: saucepan
Serves: 6

Imperial	Metric
1 large pineapple	1 large pineapple
about 1 lb. mixed fruits, grapes, fresh or frozen raspberries or strawberries, blackberries, segments of orange, diced ripe pears	about ½ kg. mixed fruits, grapes, fresh or frozen raspberries or strawberries, blackberries, segments of orange, diced ripe pears
Syrup:	*Syrup:*
approximately ¼ pint white wine	approximately 125 ml. white wine
1 tablespoon honey	1 tablespoon honey
2 tablespoons Kirsch	2 tablespoons Kirsch

1. Cut the stalk end from the pineapple.
2. Remove all the pulp and dice this neatly.
3. Slit the grapes and take out the pips, skin if liked.
4. If using frozen fruit allow this to defrost, but do not let it become too soft, otherwise it loses both flavour and texture.
5. Cut the skin away from the orange so the outer pith is also removed, and cut the segments to discard skin and pips; prepare pears last to keep them a good colour.
6. Mix all the fruit with the pineapple and cover with syrup.
7. To make this heat the ingredients slowly in a saucepan.
8. Pile back into the pineapple case.
9. Serve chilled with cream or ice cream.

Variation

Canned fruit salad can be used in place of the mixed fresh fruits. The canned syrup can be used instead of the one above.

Melon basket

Preparation time: 20 minutes
Main utensil: large basin
Serves: 6

Imperial	Metric
1 medium melon (canteloup is ideal)	1 medium melon (canteloup is ideal)
about 1 lb. mixed fresh fruit as available (see note)	about $\frac{1}{2}$ kg. mixed fresh fruit as available (see note)
squeeze lemon juice	squeeze lemon juice
little sugar	little sugar
little sherry or Kirsch (optional)	little sherry or Kirsch (optional)
To decorate:	*To decorate:*
fresh mint or bay leaves	fresh mint or bay leaves

1. Cut a slice from one end of the melon, making sure the case is standing level.

2. Remove and discard the seeds.

3. Dice the melon flesh or make into balls with a vegetable scoop.

4. Put into a basin with the fruit.

5. Grapes should be de-pipped, pear peeled, diced or sliced and dipped in lemon juice to keep it white. Grapefruit should be divided into small segments, all pith and pips removed. Halve large strawberries, remove pith and pips from orange segments — kumquats (when available) should be kept whole to give colour.

6. Mix with sugar, sherry or Kirsch, pile back into the melon case. Decorate with mint or bay leaves. Serve chilled with cream.

Note: The melon in the picture was filled with grapes, strawberries, dessert pear, grapefruit and kumquats.

Variation

Fill the bottom of the melon case with ice cream and top with melon balls.

Frosted fruit

Preparation time: 10 minutes
Main utensil: fine pastry brush
Serves: 4–6

Imperial	Metric
approximately 8 oz. fruit (see note)	approximately 200 g. fruit (see note)
1 egg white	1 egg white
approximately 3 tablespoons castor sugar	approximately 3 tablespoons castor sugar

1. Prepare the fruit, remove the stalks, but leave grapes in tiny neat bunches, wash and dry thoroughly.

2. Remove the pith and pips from orange segments without spoiling the shape.

3. Leave redcurrants and blackcurrants in bunches where possible.

4. Rinse away surplus syrup from glacé cherries, leave fresh cherries on stalks.

5. Beat the egg white very lightly with a fork, do not attempt to make it white and frothy. Brush the fruit with this.

6. Either dust the fruit with castor sugar from a fine sifter or dip in sugar.

7. Leave to dry in a warm place for several hours, then serve.

Note: Use white and black grapes; soft fruit such as red, black or white currants; glacé cherries or fresh cherries.

Almond and chocolate gâteau

Main utensils: cake tin and greaseproof paper same diameter as cake
Serves: 8–10

Imperial	Metric
1 8-inch plain sponge cake	1 20-cm. plain sponge cake
generous $\frac{1}{4}$ pint very strong black coffee	generous 125 ml. very strong black coffee
1–2 tablespoons Tia Maria	1–2 tablespoons Tia Maria
Filling:	*Filling:*
3 oz. butter	75 g. butter
3 oz. icing sugar, sieved	75 g. icing sugar, sieved
1 egg yolk	1 egg yolk
2–3 oz. ground almonds	50–75 g. ground almonds
1–1$\frac{1}{2}$ oz. cocoa	25–40 g. cocoa
1–2 tablespoons strong black coffee	1–2 tablespoons strong black coffee
To decorate:	*To decorate:*
$\frac{1}{4}$ pint double cream	125 ml. double cream
1 oz. icing sugar, sieved	25 g. icing sugar, sieved
1 egg white	1 egg white
1–2 tablespoons Tia Maria	1–2 tablespoons Tia Maria
few chopped browned almonds	few chopped browned almonds
little grated chocolate	little grated chocolate
few meringues (optional, see below)	few meringues (optional, see below)

1. Put the paper into the tin. Cut the cake into three layers, put one into the tin.

2. Mix the coffee and Tia Maria, moisten the bottom layer of cake.

3. Cream the butter, add all ingredients for filling to give a soft consistency; spread half over the cake.

4. Cover with second layer of cake, moisten with coffee and cover with the remaining chocolate almond mixture.

5. Put on the third cake layer, using the remainder of the coffee to moisten this.

6. Cover with a plate, leave for several hours, or 1–2 days in the refrigerator, then turn out on to a serving plate.

7. Whip the cream, fold in the sugar. Whip the egg white stiffly and fold in to the cream with the Tia Maria.

8. Spread most of the cream mixture over the cake. Pipe the remainder on top.

9. Decorate with nuts, chocolate and meringues.

To make meringues

Whisk 1 egg white very stiffly, gradually beat in 1 oz. (25 g.) sugar, then fold in 1 oz. (25 g.) sugar; pipe or spoon on to oiled tin. Dry out for several hours in a very cool oven (225°F., 110°C., Gas Mark 0–$\frac{1}{4}$).

French apple flan

Cooking time: 25 minutes
Preparation time: 25 minutes
Main cooking utensils: 7–8-inch (18–20-cm.) fluted flan ring,
    baking tray, saucepan
Oven temperature: hot (425°F., 220°C., Gas Mark 7)
Oven position: centre
Serves: 6

Imperial

Flan or fleur pastry:
3 oz. butter or margarine
1 oz. sugar
6 oz. plain flour
1 egg yolk
cold water
Filling:
1½ lb. apples, peeled and
    sliced (see note)
little sugar
4 tablespoons apricot jam

Metric

Flan or fleur pastry:
75 g. butter or margarine
25 g. sugar
150 g. plain flour
1 egg yolk
cold water
Filling:
¾ kg. apples, peeled and
    sliced (see note)
little sugar
4 tablespoons apricot jam

1. Cream the butter and sugar until really soft and light.
2. Add the flour and work together with a palette knife.
3. Stir in the egg yolk and sufficient water to make a rolling consistency.
4. Roll out on a lightly floured board.
5. Fit into the ring or tin, trim edges and bake blind for 10 minutes only. (Place greaseproof paper in the pastry case and fill with baking beans.)
6. Meanwhile, simmer some of the apples with sugar to give thick purée — spread over the half-cooked pastry.
7. Cover with wafer-thin slices of apple and a little sugar, return to the oven until the pastry is brown and apples tender.
8. Cover with melted apricot jam and serve with cream.

Note: To keep apples white, place peeled slices in cold water to which a little lemon juice or salt has been added.

Variation
Use other fruit in place of the apples.

Polish rich chocolate gâteau

Cooking time: 45–50 minutes
Preparation time: 30 minutes
Main cooking utensils: 8-inch (20-cm.) sandwich tin, small tin
Oven temperature: moderate (325–350°F., 170–180°C., Gas
  Mark 3–4)
Oven position: centre and above centre
Serves: 8–10

Imperial	Metric
Cake:	*Cake:*
4 large eggs	4 standard eggs
4 oz. castor sugar	100 g. castor sugar
4 oz. ground almonds	100 g. ground almonds
4 oz. plain chocolate	100 g. plain chocolate
Topping:	*Topping:*
½ pint thick cream	250 ml. thick cream
1 tablespoon rum or brandy	1 tablespoon rum or brandy
cake crumbs (see stage 6)	cake crumbs (see stage 6)
Icing:	*Icing:*
4 oz. plain chocolate	100 g. plain chocolate
1 tablespoon black coffee	1 scant tablespoon black coffee
¼ oz. butter	10 g. butter
To decorate:	*To decorate:*
whole blanched almonds	whole blanched almonds

1. Put the eggs and sugar into a large bowl; whisk until thick. The mark of the whisk should show in the mixture.
2. Fold in the ground almonds, then the chocolate — melted over hot water.
3. Put three-quarters of the mixture into a greased sandwich tin, put rest into a small greased tin to use for crumbs.
4. Bake the cake in the centre of the oven and the small cake above this.
5. Remove the small cake after approximately 25 minutes and cook the large cake for the given time.
6. Keep until the next day, make crumbs from the small cake.
7. Whisk cream until just stiff, fold in rum or brandy and crumbs.
8. Spread smoothly around the top edge of the cake.
9. Melt the chocolate for the icing with coffee and butter over hot water.
10. Allow to cool but remain soft, then spoon over the top of the cake, spreading it evenly.
11. Decorate with almonds and serve as a dessert or for tea.

Variation
Use ground hazelnuts in place of the almonds.

Melbourne apricot gâteau

Preparation time: 20 minutes
Serves: 6–8

Imperial	Metric
4 oz. butter	100 g. butter
4 oz. icing sugar	100 g. icing sugar
2 oz. castor sugar	50 g. castor sugar
1 medium can apricot halves	1 medium can apricot halves
grated rind of 1 lemon	grated rind of 1 lemon
12 sponge fingers	12 sponge fingers
To decorate:	*To decorate:*
1 oz. flaked browned almonds (see note)	25 g. flaked browned almonds (see note)

1. Cream the butter with the icing and castor sugar until soft and creamy.

2. Drain the apricots.

3. Stir 1 tablespoon apricot syrup and grated lemon rind into the butter mixture.

4. Dip six sponge fingers in remaining apricot syrup and arrange on a serving plate side by side.

5. Spread lightly with the butter cream mixture.

6. Chop half the apricots and arrange on top pressing lightly into the butter cream.

7. Dip remaining sponge fingers in syrup and arrange on top.

8. Top with butter cream and cover with rest of the reserved apricot halves.

9. Spike with almonds and chill for 30 minutes before serving.

10. Serve cut down through the sponge fingers in slices.

Note : Blanch the almonds (see page 125). Split them, and brown gently under the grill or in a moderate oven.

Variation
Other canned fruit, such as pineapple or peaches, can be used instead of the apricots.

Raspberry almond shortcake

Cooking time: 20–30 minutes
Preparation time: 20 minutes
Main cooking utensil: greased baking sheet or tin
Oven temperature: moderate (325–350°F., 170–180°C.,
   Gas Mark 3–4)
Oven position: centre
Serves: 6

Imperial	Metric
6 oz. plain flour	150 g. plain flour
4 oz. margarine	100 g. margarine
3 oz. ground almonds	75 g. ground almonds
3 oz. castor sugar	75 g. castor sugar
1 egg yolk to bind	1 egg yolk to bind
To decorate:	*To decorate:*
¼ pint double cream	125 ml. double cream
sugar to taste	sugar to taste
icing sugar	icing sugar
1 medium punnet raspberries	1 medium punnet raspberries

1. Sieve the flour into the mixing bowl.

2. Rub in the margarine until the mixture resembles fine breadcrumbs.

3. Stir in the ground almonds and sugar.

4. Add the yolk of egg, mix together lightly but firmly.

5. Turn on to a lightly floured board and roll out fairly thinly.

6. Cut in three 6-inch (15-cm.) rounds and place on a well greased baking sheet.

7. Bake for time given.

8. Cool on a wire tray.

9. Whisk the cream until stiff. Sweeten.

10. Sandwich the layers with most of the cream. Sprinkle the top with icing sugar and decorate with remaining cream and the raspberries.

Note: The shortcake can be kept for 2–3 days in an airtight tin before decorating.

Midsummer gâteau

Cooking time: 15–20 minutes
Preparation time: 25–30 minutes
Main cooking utensils: two 6-inch (15-cm.) sandwich tins (rather
  deep ones) or two 7-inch (18-cm.) shallow tins
Oven temperature: moderately hot (375–400°F., 190–200°C.,
  Gas Mark 5–6)
Oven position: above centre

Imperial	**Metric**
3 eggs	3 eggs
4 oz. castor sugar	100 g. castor sugar
2½ oz. self-raising flour	65 g. self-raising flour
(or plain flour with ½	(or plain flour with ½
teaspoon baking powder)	teaspoon baking powder)
½ oz. cocoa	15 g. cocoa
Filling:	*Filling:*
½ pint thick cream	250 ml. thick cream
12 oz.–1 lb. strawberries	350–450 g. strawberries
little sugar	little sugar

1. Whisk the eggs and sugar until thick. Fold in the sieved dry ingredients.

2. Pour into the well greased and floured or lined sandwich tins.

3. Bake for time given — the 7-inch (18-cm.) cakes take a few minutes less than the deeper 6-inch (15-cm.) cakes.

4. Test to see if cooked — when cooked they should be firm to the touch.

5. Turn out carefully and cool.

6. Split each cake through the centre.

7. Whip the cream until it holds its shape, but is not too stiff.

8. Spread between the cakes with the sliced or halved fruit and sugar to taste.

9. Top with the cream and whole strawberries and serve as a dessert or for tea.

Variation

Use 3 oz. (75 g.) flour and omit the cocoa. Fill with other fresh or well drained canned or frozen fruits as available.

Dreamy Swiss roll

Cooking time: 7–10 minutes
Preparation time: 15 minutes
Main cooking utensil: lined Swiss roll tin
Oven temperature: moderately hot to hot (400–425°F., 200–220°C., Gas Mark 6–7)
Oven position: near top
Serves: 8

Imperial

3 large eggs
3–4 oz. castor sugar
3 oz. flour (plain or self-raising)
1 tablespoon hot water
Filling:
4–6 tablespoons warm
  strawberry jam or defrosted
  or well drained canned
  strawberries
Coating:
1 packet dream topping
6–7 tablespoons milk
To decorate:
1–2 tablespoons jam or few
  well drained strawberries

Metric

3 large eggs
75–100 g. castor sugar
75 g. flour (plain or self-raising)
1 tablespoon hot water
Filling:
4–6 tablespoons warm
  strawberry jam or defrosted
  or well drained canned
  strawberries
Coating:
1 packet dream topping
6–7 tablespoons milk
To decorate:
1–2 tablespoons jam or few
  well drained strawberries

1. Put the eggs and sugar into a large mixing bowl, and whisk until the mixture is thick and creamy (you see the trail of the whisk); if done over hot water, continue beating until the mixture cools again.

2. Sieve the flour at least once.

3. Fold gently into the egg mixture with a metal spoon. Lastly, fold in the water.

4. Pour into the lined, greased tin.

5. Bake for time and temperature given.

6. Test before removing from oven — press with finger, if no impression remains, the cake is cooked.

7. Turn on to sugared paper, spread with jam or strawberries, roll firmly.

8. For the coating, whisk the dream topping into cold milk until fluffy and thick, spread over the cold Swiss roll.

9. Decorate with jam or strawberries.

Ice cream with coffee butterscotch sauce

Cooking time: few minutes for sauce
Preparation time: 8 minutes
Main cooking utensils: freezing tray, saucepan
Serves: 4–6

Imperial	Metric
2 eggs	2 eggs
2 oz. icing sugar, sieved	50 g. icing sugar, sieved
¼ pint whipped cream or whipped evaporated milk (see note)	125 ml. whipped cream or whipped evaporated milk (see note)
flavouring (see variation)	flavouring (see variation)
Sauce:	*Sauce:*
3 oz. butter	75 g. butter
6 oz. soft brown sugar	150 g. soft brown sugar
3 tablespoons single cream	3 tablespoons single cream
2 tablespoons coffee essence	2 tablespoons coffee essence

1. Before freezing home made ice cream always turn the cold control indicator to the coldest position for 30 minutes before putting in the mixture.

2. Separate the egg yolks from the whites.

3. Beat the yolks with sugar, then fold in the lightly whipped cream, flavouring and the stiffly beaten egg whites.

4. Put into the freezing tray and leave until just firm, return the indicator to its normal setting.

5. To make the sauce, melt the butter in a strong saucepan, add the sugar and stir until dissolved, then add the cream and essence. Bring to the boil and cook for 2 minutes.

6. Spoon the ice cream into sundae glasses and serve the sauce, hot or cold, separately.

Note: To whip evaporated milk, boil the can for 15 minutes. Open carefully and allow milk to cool. Whisk until stiff. (For a stiffer consistency dissolve 1 teaspoon powdered gelatine in the hot milk.)

Variations

The ice cream can be flavoured with the addition of a few drops of vanilla essence, or 2 oz. (50 g.) chocolate powder, or 1–2 tablespoons coffee essence (beaten with the egg yolks), or 4–6 tablespoons fruit purée.

Pots au chocolat

Cooking time: few minutes
Preparation time: 10 minutes
Main cooking utensil: double saucepan or basin over hot water
Serves: 4–6

Imperial	**Metric**
4 oz. chocolate, preferably plain	100 g. chocolate, preferably plain
1 oz. butter	25 g. butter
2 eggs	2 eggs
4 oz. marshmallows	100 g. marshmallows
1 tablespoon hot water	1 tablespoon hot water
To decorate:	*To decorate:*
grated chocolate	grated chocolate

1. Put the chocolate, broken into small pieces into the top of the double saucepan or basin, and melt over hot water.
2. Add the butter, egg yolks and the marshmallows and cook, stirring well, until the marshmallows have melted and mixture is smooth and shiny.
3. Add the water, stir well, then allow the mixture to cool, but not set.
4. Whisk the egg whites until very stiff, fold into the chocolate mixture, then put into 4 or 6 individual dishes.
5. When quite cold decorate with grated chocolate.
6. Serve with plain biscuits or fingers of sponge.

Variation
Use coffee essence or strong black coffee in place of the water.

Coffee party mousse

Cooking time: few minutes to heat water
Preparation time: 20 minutes
Main utensil: 6–7-inch (15–18-cm.) cake tin or mould
Serves: 6–8

Imperial	Metric
$\frac{1}{2}$ oz. powdered gelatine (1 level tablespoon)	15 g. powdered gelatine (1 level tablespoon)
$\frac{1}{4}$ pint hot water	125 ml. hot water
3 tablespoons coffee essence	3 tablespoons coffee essence
3 egg yolks	3 egg yolks
2 oz. castor sugar	50 g. castor sugar
$\frac{1}{4}$ pint double cream	125 ml. double cream
3 egg whites	3 egg whites
To decorate:	*To decorate:*
8 oz. sponge finger biscuits	200 g. sponge finger biscuits
2–3 tablespoons double cream	2–3 tablespoons double cream
8 hazelnuts or walnut halves	8 hazelnuts or walnut halves

1. Dissolve the gelatine in the water, blend with the coffee essence.

2. Beat the egg yolks and sugar in a basin over a pan of simmering water until thick and creamy.

3. Remove and gradually beat in the coffee and gelatine mixture.

4. When cold (but not set) fold in the lightly whipped cream.

5. Beat egg whites until stiff, fold into the coffee mixture.

6. Pour into a cake tin or mould and chill until firm.

7. To turn out dip the cake tin in hot water for 4–5 seconds and invert on to a flat dish.

8. Trim the sponge fingers to the height of the mousse and set them all the way round it.

9. Decorate the top with the blobs or piped whirls of cream and place the nuts on top. Serve with cream or ice cream.

Coffee soufflé

Cooking time: few minutes to soften gelatine
Preparation time: 25 minutes
Main cooking utensils: saucepan, 5-inch (13-cm.) soufflé dish,
   greaseproof paper
Serves: 4

Imperial	Metric
4 oz. flour	100 g. flour
2 oz. breadcrumbs	50 g. breadcrumbs
1 teaspoon mixed spice	1 teaspoon mixed spice
1 level teaspoon cinnamon	1 level teaspoon cinnamon
1 level teaspoon nutmeg	1 level teaspoon nutmeg
4 oz. shredded suet	100 g. shredded suet
4 oz. brown sugar	100 g. brown sugar
4 oz. grated apple	100 g. grated apple
1 small carrot, grated	1 small carrot, grated
4 oz. mixed crystallised peel	100 g. mixed crystallised peel
4 oz. currants	100 g. currants
8 oz. raisins	200 g. raisins
4 oz. sultanas	100 g. sultanas
2 oz. prunes or dried apricots, chopped	50 g. prunes or dried apricots, chopped
4 oz. almonds, blanched and chopped	100 g. almonds, blanched and chopped
grated rind of $\frac{1}{2}$ lemon	grated rind of $\frac{1}{2}$ lemon
juice of $\frac{1}{2}$ lemon	juice of $\frac{1}{2}$ lemon
grated rind of $\frac{1}{2}$ orange	grated rind of $\frac{1}{2}$ orange
1 tablespoon golden syrup or black treacle	1 tablespoon golden syrup or black treacle
$\frac{1}{4}$ pint ale, beer or milk	125 ml. ale, beer or milk
2 eggs	2 eggs
Brandy butter:	*Brandy butter:*
4 oz. butter	100 g. butter
6 oz. icing sugar	150 g. icing sugar
2 tablespoons brandy	2 tablespoons brandy

1. Mix all the ingredients together and leave overnight, then stir again, wishing hard for good luck.

2. Put into the greased basin or basins, cover with foil, greaseproof paper or a cloth. It is a good idea to grease both the inside and outside of the paper to keep the pudding dry on top — or cover with a flour and water paste (mix 8 oz. (200 g.) flour with water).

3. Steam or boil for time given, allowing longer time for one pudding. Remove the wet covers as soon as the pudding is cooked, then put on dry covers and re-steam for 2—3 hours on Christmas morning.

4. Cream the butter and icing sugar together for the brandy butter. Beat in the brandy.

5. Serve the Christmas pudding with the brandy butter.

Note: If it is necessary to wash your fruit for a Christmas pudding or cake, allow it to dry for 48 hours in room temperature before using. Keep the made pudding in a cool dry place.

Glogg

Cooking time: few minutes
Preparation time: few minutes
Main cooking utensil: large saucepan
Serves: 8–10

Imperial	Metric
1 bottle red wine (Margaux, St. Emilon, Beaune, Beaujolais etc.)	1 bottle red wine (Margaux, St. Emilon, Beaune, Beaujolais etc.)
$\frac{1}{4}$ pint gin	125 ml. gin
1 stick cinnamon	1 stick cinnamon
10 cloves	10 cloves
2–3 oz. almonds, blanched (see note)	50–75 g. almonds, blanched (see note)
5 oz. seedless raisins	125 g. seedless raisins
1 tablespoon clear honey	1 tablespoon clear honey

1. Put the glasses to warm, as this drink must be served very hot.

2. Open the wine and pour it carefully into the pan; should there be any sediment at the bottom of the bottle avoid this.

3. Add the gin, cinnamon and cloves. The cinnamon can be bruised slightly to bring out more of its flavour.

4. Simmer gently for a few minutes, then remove from the heat and add the almonds, raisins and honey.

5. Cool for 2–3 minutes only, then pour into the glasses. If a spoon is put into each glass as the drink is poured in, there is less chance of any glass cracking.

6. Serve as a party drink.

Note: To blanch almonds, put them into boiling water for $\frac{1}{2}$ minute, then drain. When cool enough to handle, remove the skins.

Variation

If liked, use less cloves or remove them after heating the ingredients so that the flavour is less pronounced.

Claret punch

Cooking time: 10 minutes
Preparation time: 5 minutes
Main cooking utensil: saucepan
Serves: 12–18

Imperial	Metric
1½ pints water	scant 1 litre water
6 oz. sugar	150 g. sugar
rind of 2 lemons	rind of 2 lemons
juice of 2 lemons	juice of 2 lemons
2 bottles claret	2 bottles claret
½ pint inexpensive port	250 ml. inexpensive port
1 stick cinnamon	1 stick cinnamon
Mulled ale:	*Mulled ale:*
2 pints good ale	1 litre good ale
1 glass rum or brandy	1 glass rum or brandy
1 tablespoon sugar	1 tablespoon sugar
pinch ground cloves	pinch ground cloves
pinch powdered ginger	pinch powdered ginger

1. Put the water and sugar into the pan and boil for 5 minutes.
2. Add the lemon rind, lemon juice, claret, port and the stick of cinnamon.
3. Heat for a few minutes, then strain into a hot punch bowl.
4. For the mulled ale, heat all the ingredients together but do not allow to boil.
5. Serve in warm glasses.

Variation
Spiced punch: Omit the claret and port, use ½ pint (250 ml.) brandy, ½ pint (250 ml.) rum and flavour with mixed spice as well as cinnamon.

Acknowledgements

The following photographs are by courtesy of:

Atora: pages 72, 122
Beecham Foods Limited: page 118
Cadbury Schweppes Foods Limited: page 104
Christian Délu: pages 82, 84
Fruit Producers' Council: pages 34, 88, 90, 96, 126
Gales Honey: page 124
Green Giant: page 64
Michael Holford: page 66
Isleworth Polytechnic: pages 16, 38
Italian Institute: pages 30, 32, 80
Mazola: page 54
George Newnes Limited: pages 94, 120
RHM Foods Limited: pages 78, 92
White Fish Authority: page 42

Hamlyn all-colour cookbooks

Party Fare

Marguerite Patten

Hamlyn
London · New York · Sydney · Toronto

Published by
The Hamlyn Publishing Group Limited
London · New York · Sydney · Toronto
Hamlyn House, Feltham, Middlesex, England
© Copyright The Hamlyn Publishing Group Limited 1973
ISBN 0 600 30200 8
Printed in England by Sir Joseph Causton and Sons Limited
Line drawings by John Scott Martin